Praying Through Baby's First Year

Nicole Gibelyou

DEDICATION

To all priests who are docile to the Spirit and who make Jesus present to us in the confessional. Receiving a penance of reflecting on God's presence in motherhood confirmed a project which had recently been written on my heart – to write the daily prayers and reflections that I had in taking care of my son.

To my friends and family who were giving birth around the time this was written. This book was written with you in mind.

To my husband and family who have always encouraged me to write and who are my primary editors.

And to my son, out of whose mouth is brought forth perfect praise (Matthew 21:16).

INTRODUCTION

I expected praying while raising an infant to be difficult due to time constraints. What I did not expect was that it would be physically impossible. With frequent night wakings, I was too physically and mentally exhausted for meditative prayer. "Mom brain" became a very real thing. I lost the ability to think clearly. Anytime I closed my eyes, I slipped into a dreamlike state, and most of the silence was filled with thoughts of how I was failing as a mother. I felt frustrated and spiritually dry. I was convinced that there must be a way to grow spiritually in every season of life, especially during the beautiful and life-changing (albeit stressful) season of becoming a mother, but I did not know how.

I needed a structured way of praying in order to stay focused, a way of praying that would allow me to meditate on my new life as a mother. Over the first several months of raising my son, I developed the format described in the pages that follow. This format took shape for me as I sought to naturally integrate meditative prayer into my everyday life as a new parent. I found that meditating on how the relationship between my child and me reflected my relationship with God the Father helped to focus my awareness of God's presence in every aspect of my life. The prayer format is as follows:

Heavenly Father...

The prayers are directed as a spiritual child to our spiritual Father who lovingly cares for us. Being a "spiritual" Father does not make God less of a father than one's physical father. On the contrary, God "transcends human fatherhood...no one is father as God is Father" (CCC 239): "call none your father upon earth; for one is your father, who is in heaven" (Matthew 23:9).

I watch...

The prayer begins by observing our surroundings and letting their meaning penetrate our souls. This is akin to how Mary reflected on the events of her life in her heart: "Mary kept all these words, pondering them in her heart" (Luke 2:19).

And so I think it is with me.

Using this line adapted from Pierre Teilhard de Chardin's *Patient Trust*, we then relate the child's behavior to our own behavior, recognizing that we are all children in the spiritual life. In Baptism, we are born into the spiritual life and are invited to grow in faith. Watching our children grow provides insight into how we can grow. It also increases our empathy for our children as we recognize that in various aspects of our spiritual lives, we are no further along developmentally than our children: "As a father hath compassion on his children, so hath the Lord compassion on them that fear him" (Psalm 102:13).

Father...

We again address God as our Father and make explicit what He was teaching us in our observations. This also makes the lesson more concrete for ourselves, which can help us remember it.

Increase my...

The virtues and habits we develop to grow spiritually are given freely as gifts if we ask for them and dispose ourselves to receive them. Sometimes we work hard to obtain these gifts, but we forget to ask for them. Let God be the provider of the gift and thank Him by exercising and using the gift wisely: "in all things whatsoever you shall ask in prayer, believing, you shall receive" (Matthew 21:22).

Help me to know...

We often learn something one day and forget it the next. Here, we ask God to help us internalize what He is trying to communicate to us about Himself through our observations.

...is Your delight.

As parents, we delight in caring for our children and watching them grow. This serves as a reminder that God cares for us with even more abundant love than we offer our children, and that to watch us grow spiritually is His delight.

The rest of the book provides examples of this style of prayer; they were written shortly after they occurred to me as I was raising my son during the first year of his life. May this format and these examples provide the tool and inspiration you need to begin praying in this way as you watch your child grow and you recognize God touching your life through theirs.

Fist for Comfort

Heavenly Father,

I watch my frustrated son put his fist in his mouth while I'm trying to feed him. He complains when I remove it. I'm trying to give him the nourishment that he needs, but he prefers his hand and can't understand why he isn't satisfied. Not only does his fist not sustain him, but it actively prevents me from helping him receive what he really wants and needs.

And so I think it is with me.

Father, You freely offer me Your grace, but I instead turn to what is comfortable and actively block myself from receiving You more fully into my life. Increase my trust that You are the provider of not only my needs, but the deepest desires of my heart. Help me to know that I am Your child, and that to lavish good gifts on Your daughter is Your delight.

Amen.

Tummy Time

Heavenly Father,

I watch my son struggle as I place him on his stomach on the floor. He screams and fights with his uncoordinated legs and arms randomly jutting out. I am told that it is important for his development that I put him through this torture. It will make him stronger, especially his neck, so he will be able to lift his head, and eventually sit up and crawl. But he doesn't appreciate any of that and he probably never will. He just wants me to pick him up.

And so I think it is with me.

Father, help me to recognize that even in situations when I feel that I am not moving forward, the spiritual desert I am experiencing is making me stronger. Increase my trust that You allow unpleasant situations for a reason, and that when I reach my limit, You are right there, ready to lift me up. Help me to know that seeing me grow stronger is Your delight.

Amen.

Provider

Heavenly Father,

I watch my son as he kicks and screams to complain that he's hungry. I hold him in one arm as I prepare his bottle with the other. His movements are so vigorous that I almost knock over his bottle. When I briefly stop feeding him to readjust how he's positioned in order to help him swallow better, he cries and screams.

And so I think it is with me.

Father, teach me patience that I may wait for the daily bread You have prepared for me. Increase my trust that You are preparing it, holding me all the while, and that what You provide is the best spiritual nourishment. Help me know that seeing me accept Your gifts and thrive is Your delight.

Amen.

Carried

Heavenly Father,

I watch my son as I bring him from place to place after letting him sleep in his car seat. How confused he must be to fall asleep in one place and wake up to find himself in another. His experiences must feel disjointed. But at least when he wakes up, he finds comfort in seeing the familiar face of his parent carrying him.

And so I think it is with me.

Father, I don't always understand the meaning behind where I find myself each day. Increase my ability to see the connection between the different circumstances that I find myself in, to see everything from Your perspective. Help me to know that You are there carrying me each step of the way and that being alongside me through it all is Your delight.

Amen.

Pure Joy

Heavenly Father,

I try to get my son to laugh. I make funny noises, funny faces, try to play games that I think he'll like. He laughs at things I don't expect, which makes it even more exciting to hear. He never seems to laugh at the same thing twice. He won't laugh just to please me. He only laughs when he is sincerely overflowing with joy and can't contain that joy. He must share it. And his pure joy is contagious.

And so I wish it were with me.

Father, may my laughter not be artificial in order to please others; may I be genuinely filled with joy that overflows into laughter. Increase my integrity, that my laugh may be more authentic, and increase my ability to experience joy in the given moment without worrying about whether that joy will be taken away from me in the next. Help me to know that hearing my pure laugh is Your delight.

Amen.

Nightmare

Heavenly Father,

I watch my son as I try to comfort him through a nightmare. He wails as I hold him. I bounce him gently and whisper softly, trying to comfort him, but with little success. He continues to cry as he tries to wake himself, but he struggles to open his eyes. When he finally manages to wake fully, he gives me the broadest smile.

And so I think it is with me.

Father, I often find myself distracted by the nightmare and fail to see the greater reality, that You are holding me through everything. Increase my trust that I am always in Your arms and that You care for me. Help me to know that carrying me through all of life's moments is Your delight.

Amen.

Wonder

Heavenly Father,

I watch my son as he studies his hands so attentively. He makes careful movements, observing what happens as he makes different motions. Does he know his hands are his? Does he know the potential he has, and what he will someday learn to do?

And so I wish it were with me.

Father, return to me the wonder in my abilities that I once had. Increase my understanding that You are the giver of my abilities, which have greater potential to accomplish Your purposes than I could ever imagine. Help me to know that watching me wonder at and grow in the abilities You have given me is Your delight.

Amen.

Cleansing

Heavenly Father,

My son is frightened of bath time. I am told that many babies find bath time relaxing, but not my son. From the time the water turns on until he is taken out of the tub, his face is plastered with fear. When bath time is over, he babbles to me his joy of having survived.

And so I think it is with me.

Father, You have given me the great gift of Baptism, where I have been reborn in You through the waters of this Sacrament; I am cleansed each time I come to You for forgiveness from my sins, but I hate confessing. Increase my trust in Your mercy that I may see the love with which You love me and wash me clean time and again. Help me to know that seeing me return to You, even though I fight doing so, and allowing You to wash me clean is Your delight.

Amen.

Joy of Being

Heavenly Father,

What joy I feel as I watch my son. I rejoice when he sleeps. I rejoice when he wakes. I rejoice when he eats. I rejoice when he burps. I rejoice when he dirties his diaper. I rejoice when he coos. I rejoice when he grabs my finger. I rejoice when he struggles to roll over. I rejoice when he reaches for his toys. I rejoice, because he is fully being who he is at this moment.

And so I think it is with You.

Father, I strive to live authentically, to live each moment fully. Increase my belief that You watch me with overflowing love at each stage of my spiritual development. Help me to know that whether awake or asleep, eating or brushing my teeth, working or resting, watching me thrive as Your child is Your delight.

Amen.

Dependence

Heavenly Father,

I look at my son, so small and helpless. He depends on me for all his basic needs. He cries for me to feed him. He cries for me to put him to sleep. He cries for me if he is too warm. Too cold. Bored. Wants to be cuddled. He cries not just because he is upset, but because he knows his cry will be answered.

And so I wish it were with me.

Father, give me the grace to be humble like an infant, so I know to cry out to You for all that I need and desire. Increase my trust that You will answer my cries. Help me to know that caring for me is Your delight.

Amen.

Discomfort

Heavenly Father,

I watch my son cry from discomfort. He is filled with gas. I try to help him to relieve some of his pain by pumping his legs and bouncing him up and down to help him relax, but I am unable to get rid of it all for him. He'll have to wait for it to resolve. Although I know his pain is temporary, it is still difficult to see him cry.

And so I think it is with You.

Father, remind me that all the discomfort and pain I experience is temporary and will pass. Increase my trust that You are there with me in my distress. Help me to know that accompanying me through my pain is Your delight.

Amen.

Monotony

Heavenly Father,

I watch my son go through the same routine multiple times a day. Wake, diaper change, playtime, feed, read, playtime, feed, rock, sleep. An hour later, he goes through it again. And again. And again until he's down for the night. He doesn't mind the repetition. In fact, he thrives when he's in his routine; it allows him to learn and grow more easily. He gets disoriented and overtired when his routine is thrown off.

And so I think it is with me.

Father, thank You for the monotony of daily life, for helping me stay rooted through the mundane. Increase my ability to recognize how I may grow each day through my routine. Help me to know that meeting me in my daily routine is Your delight.

Amen.

Growing

Heavenly Father,

I watch my son learn how to grasp smaller objects. Then larger soft objects. Then larger hard objects. I watch him unable to bat at the mobile dangling over his head. Then randomly hit it occasionally. Then masterfully control exactly when he hits what. He is learning so much every day, it is incredible. But he still gets frustrated by all that he is unable to do.

And so I think it is with me.

Father, help me to recognize when I am growing spiritually. Increase my patience that I may see myself not as an expert, but as a student in my spiritual journey. Help me to know that watching me learn and grow more and more each day is Your delight.

Amen.

Discontent

Heavenly Father,

I put my son on the floor to play with his toy. He plays for five minutes before crying from boredom. I put him in his bouncy chair. He cries shortly thereafter. I put him in his swing. He cries. I read him books. Cries. He never stays content with an activity for long. We continue to cycle through the activities until he goes to bed.

And so I think it is with me.

Father, I get so restless with what I do throughout the day. Increase my desire for silence, that I may not need to be constantly entertained, and that I may be able to listen to You. Help me to know that being with me in the stillness is Your delight.

Amen.

Loved

Heavenly Father,

My son screams at me from the changing table without explanation. I smile and speak to him with what patience I have. While I'm feeding him, he pulls the nipple away from his mouth and starts screaming. I rock him gently and keep my cool the best I can. With each complaint, I choose to respond with love.

And so I think it is with You.

Father, I complain repeatedly, because I am upset; sometimes, I don't even know why I'm upset. Increase my trust that You care intimately about my life and that You will always respond with abounding, unconditional love and infinite patience. Help me to know that filling me with an outpouring of love in all situations is Your delight.

Amen.

Control

Heavenly Father,

My son sticks everything he can get his hands on in his mouth. He has plenty of toys, which are fine for him to chew on; but there are other things, like my hair or grass or dirt, that I pull from his grasping hands before they make it to his mouth. When I take away something that he may choke on or that isn't good for him, he starts to cry. He wants full control over what he puts in his mouth.

And so I think it is with me.

Father, I want control over all aspects of my life. Increase my surrender to You, that I may trust that what You do is for my own good. Help me to know that watching me respond with trust when You remove temptations from my life is Your delight.

Amen.

Be

Heavenly Father,

I think of all the things that I need to get done: laundry, dishes, grocery shopping, house cleaning, repairs. The list goes on. Some days, I feel like I'm lucky to get dressed, let alone get everything else done that needs to be done. But I watch my son. He doesn't have an agenda. He doesn't feel like he's failed if he doesn't complete everything on a list. He lives in the moment, requesting what he needs, and simply rejoices in being.

And so I wish it were with me.

Father, my vocation as a mother has two parts: the vocation to do (which is ever at the top of my mind), and the vocation to be (which I often forget). Increase my appreciation of the magnificence of being, that I may be in awe of this wondrous mystery. Help me to know that, out of Your delight, You loved me into being so that I may delight in You in return.

Amen.

Restless

Heavenly Father,

My son won't sleep. He used to sleep, but we went on vacation, and now, he's restless at night. What can I do? I feed him, rock him, walk with him, sing to him. I do all that I can think of, whether or not it seems to make a difference. For now, I will just be with him.

And so I think it is with You.

Father, when life throws something unexpected my way, my soul becomes restless. Increase my trust that I am in Your arms during the long and difficult nights. Help me to know that being present for me through it all is Your delight.

Amen.

Patience

Heavenly Father,

I change my son's diaper after he wets it. And after he wets it again. I change my son's onesie after he spits up on it. And I change it when he spits up on it again. Many times, I feel so drained that I'm not even sure I'll get through cleaning up the first time. And then, I clean up after him again.

And so I think it is with You.

Father, thank You for Your patience with me and for always cleaning up after my messes. Increase my patience and endurance that I may exhaust myself out of love for my child and for others around me. Help me to know that caring for me, including taking care of my messes, is Your delight.

Amen.

Strangers

Heavenly Father,

I watch the faces of strangers as they see my son. There are those who ignore him, but for the most part, strangers respond to him. Most at least smile, some make faces, play peek-a-boo, or talk with him. Regardless of the attitude these strangers have before approaching him, they seem to be filled with joy once they've encountered him.

And so I wish it were with me.

Father, my son radiates Your light so effortlessly, giving everyone he meets an encounter with You. Increase Your grace within me that I may decrease, and those who meet me may meet You. Help me to know that making Yourself present to others through me is Your delight.

Amen.

Reaching for Light

Heavenly Father,

I watch my son as he reaches for every light he sees: ceiling lights, lamps, Christmas lights, nightlights, indicators on electronics. It doesn't matter if the light is within reach or not. It doesn't matter if it is large or small. He reaches for it with all his might.

And so I wish it were with me.

Father, I want to desire the light as much as my son, but I often settle for what is dim, figuring that such purity is unobtainable. Increase my yearning for the light – what is good, true, and perfect. Help me to know that seeing me striving for the light, seeking You where You may be found, and bearing Your light to others is Your delight.

Amen.

Anxiety

Heavenly Father,

I try to lull my son to sleep. I feed him. I rock him. I bounce him. But he won't settle down. He doesn't know how to soothe himself to sleep. He doesn't know how to calm himself down. And despite my efforts, he can't fall asleep. He's overtired and he cries, but all I can do is wait until he collapses from exhaustion in my arms.

And so I think it is with You.

Father, You try to relieve my anxiety. Increase my trust that You are holding me lovingly in Your arms, trying to calm me in the midst of the storms of life. Help me to know that seeing me collapse in peace in Your arms is Your delight.

Amen.

Help

Heavenly Father,

My son is learning to roll from his front to his back. He pushes himself on his side, but can't make it any farther than that. I help him by nudging him until he's on his back. When he's on his back, he looks up at me with such pride and satisfaction at having completed the turn.

And so I think it is with me.

Father, You are so gracious in granting me a sense of independence and confidence in my abilities. Increase my awareness that every success of mine is made possible with Your help and should be a beacon that points others directly to You. Help me to know that seeing me succeed and the joy it brings me is Your delight.

Amen.

Nutrition

Heavenly Father,

I watch my son as he is learning how to eat. He already has his favorite foods, namely the sweetest fruits. Not that fruits are bad, but they don't have the nutrients he needs from vegetables and other foods. So I mix the fruits with his other food to encourage him to eat it, hoping that someday, I will be able to wean him off the sweetener little by little until he enjoys the more substantial food on its own.

And so I think it is with You.

Father, hidden in all the counterfeit pleasures of life is the presence of Your reality that brings fulfillment. Increase my awareness of the times when I fall for the sweetener even though it is the substance hidden underneath that will bring me life. Help me to know that seeing me spiritually fulfilled is Your delight.

Amen.

Delayed Gratification

Heavenly Father,

I watch my son as he begs to be fed. If I feed him
now, he won't be able to fall asleep during his nap time
in 15 minutes, because he will be too full to be soothed
to sleep. But he doesn't want to wait. He cries and
screams, and I give him what he thinks he wants. When
it is time for his nap, he is unable to fall asleep. He gets
cranky, but has to wait another half hour or so before
he's ready to be calmed.

And so I think it is with me.

Father, I know what I think I want and I don't
understand why You don't give it to me now. Increase
my trust that the desire and longing that I experience is
actually for a greater good that ultimately only You can
fulfill. Help me to know that fulfilling my deepest desires
with Your unconditional love is Your delight.

Amen.

Cry

Heavenly Father,

I hear my son as he cries out for me. He doesn't cry out in pain. I'm not convinced he cries out in sorrow. It seems to me that he cries out with complete faith that I will come to him, hold him, and reassure him that he is not alone. I am there for him.

And so I think it is with me.

Father, I cry out to You at times to be reassured that You are there watching over me. Increase my trust that You are always there to answer my cries. Help me to know that soothing me when I cry out Your name is Your delight.

Amen.

Six Months

Heavenly Father,

I watch my son's progress as he turns six months. He has become a very good sitter. He reaches out and tries to grab everything. He is starting to eat puréed food. But he is frustrated. He sees us move and wants to move. He sees us eat and wants solid food. He doesn't appreciate that a mere six months ago, he couldn't even lift his own head.

And so I think it is with me.

Father, I get so impatient with my spiritual journey; I want to be perfect now. Increase my patience and my understanding that You are working in and through my imperfections. Help me to know that watching me as I progress and grow in holiness, as I grow into who You created me to be, is Your delight.

Amen.

Teething

Heavenly Father,

I watch my son as he is up way past his bedtime. He hasn't eaten right for days. He is much fussier than usual during the day. He wakes up more regularly at night. Each morning, I check eagerly to see if a tooth has erupted, only to feel nothing. We will all have to endure this jarring break from the usual routine for yet another day.

And so I think it is with me.

Father, life comes with many growing pains that not only affect us, but those around us. Increase my endurance to handle unwelcome disruptions to my routine, and increase my awareness of how each disruption helps me grow. Help me to know that watching me grow through all aspects of life, through both the usual routine and the disruptions, is Your delight.

Amen.

In His Image

Heavenly Father,

I look in my son's eyes. It is like looking into my own.
Everyone says he has his mother's eyes and her curly
hair. He has his father's chin and energy. People say that
he is a perfect mix of both parents. Although he
resembles us, because he has a mix of our genes, he is
still his own person. What a wonder to look on him who
came from our love and from my body.

And so I wonder if it is with You.

Father, You created us in Your image. Increase in me
that I may resemble You more and more, so when
people see me, they see You. Help me to know that
watching me accept Your Spirit and the graces that You
shower upon me is Your delight.

Amen.

Hard to Soothe

Heavenly Father,

I watch my son as I try to soothe him back to sleep, but tonight has been especially difficult. First, a neighbor's dog woke him. Then a car horn. And now with a siren blaring in the background, I don't know that there's much more I can do to help him than to just hold him and wait for it to pass.

And so I think it is with You.

Father, You try to comfort me during difficult times, but I'm often so distracted that I don't even recognize You're there. Increase my awareness of Your presence during difficult times. Help me to know that being there and holding me until the worst is past is Your delight.

Amen.

Little Pleasures

Heavenly Father,

I watch my son as he laughs at the little things. He giggles as he watches a Tupperware container roll along the floor. He giggles as I put his baby blanket over his head and pull it away. He giggles when I make silly noises at him. It does not take much to bring him joy.

And so I wish it were with me.

Father, You offer me so many little pleasures that I sometimes fail to enjoy, because I am overwhelmed by other things. Increase my appreciation for all the little moments that bring me joy. Help me to know that interacting with me through all the little things is Your delight.

Amen.

Eyes

Heavenly Father,

I look into the eyes of my son. How clear they are, untainted by regret, hurt, despair. They are pure windows into his soul. I wonder how similar it is for me to look into his eyes as it was for Mary to look into her Son's eyes, because in my son's eyes, I feel like I see You.

And so I wish it were with me.

Father, let my eyes be a window to You for all those who make eye contact with me. Increase the transparency of my eyes, that my fallen nature may not cloud the view others may have of You in them. Help me to know that seeing the scales fall from my eyes and restoring their vision to its original clarity is Your delight.

Amen.

Attention

Heavenly Father,

I hear my son screaming as I load the dishwasher. The moment I walk over to him, he smiles. He starts screaming as I work on cleaning the family room. When I go to him, he smiles. He screams as I read right next to him. When I look at him, he smiles. He wants nothing more than my attention.

And so I think it is with me.

Father, there are times when I just want to know that You are there caring for me. Increase my trust that I never need to compete for Your undivided attention. Help me to know that attentively watching over me is Your delight.

Amen.

Environment

Heavenly Father,

I watch my son as he makes his way around the room, moving from toy to toy. He probably thinks the room was always this way: his playthings covering the floor, bookcases secured to the wall, covers on the electrical outlets, childproof locks on the cabinets. He has never known anything different. But it wasn't until very recently that the house looked this way, and I have lived what feels like several lifetimes before he was even born.

And so I think it is with You.

Father, the habitable Earth on which we live is so new to You who were there at the dawn of space and time. Increase my wonder at how You have created a place and time for me to thrive. Help me to know that seeing me explore the world around me is Your delight.

Amen.

Distractions

Heavenly Father,

I watch my son as he cries out. I reach out my arms and call for him to crawl to me. He starts crawling in my direction, but he soon gets distracted by the toys that stand between him and me, and settles for playing with them.

And so I think it is with me.

Father, when I'm upset and cry out to You, You call me to Yourself to be comforted, but I settle for temporary pleasures that distract me from You. Increase my awareness of times when I settle for less than the comfort You provide. Help me to know that watching me turn to You as my comforter in times of distress is Your delight.

Amen.

Out of Reach

Heavenly Father,

I watch my son as he is learning how to get down from a shallow step. He places a toy at the bottom of the step and reaches down to grab it. Then he throws it. Sometimes it lands close to the bottom of the step, in which case he is able to easily reach down and grab it again. If it's too far, he'll call out to me to help him down the step so he can get the toy. But sometimes it lands just out of reach. It is when the toy is in this position that reaching for it helps my son's development the most. It challenges him to reach further than he had ever been able to do before. Sometimes he succeeds, sometimes he doesn't, but he will succeed someday. This exercise he has created for himself will help him learn more quickly.

And so I wish it were with me.

Father, I want to grow spiritually in the most effective way I can. Increase my awareness of ways in which I can challenge myself spiritually that are still within my reach. Help me to know that watching me grow step by step is Your delight.

Amen.

Security

Heavenly Father,

I watch my son as he becomes more adventurous. He crawls into other rooms. He crawls over to strangers. He climbs steps. But with every new and daring thing he does, he always looks back to make sure Mommy's there. Seeing Mommy there smiling at him, he boldly moves forward with courage to explore his world.

And so I wish it were with me.

Father, I want to know that You are with me every step of the way, but even when I see You there with me, I'm afraid to proceed. Increase my trust that You will be with me constantly through anything You call me to. Help me to know that seeing me move forward with courage because I am relying on You for security is Your delight.

Amen.

Attention to Detail

Heavenly Father,

I watch my son as he picks up little pieces of lint or crumbs that I didn't know were there. I watch his fascination with little details like raindrops or characters' eyes in his books. He sees and admires things that I don't recognize as things. He doesn't miss the fine details of his surroundings.

And so I wish it were with me.

Father, You created all things great and small, but I often fail to fully appreciate the unseen details of Your creation. Increase my ability to perceive and bask in the glory of those aspects of Your creation that are most often overlooked. Help me to know that watching my eyes light up with wonder as I gaze at Your creation is Your delight.

Amen.

Milestones

Heavenly Father,

I watch my son as he pulls himself up to a standing position for the first time. To him, it's all new. There was something in him that kept driving him to try, that inner voice that said, "this must be possible, and if it is, it would be a good thing for me to figure out." To me, it was always clear that he could do it and eventually would. It's a milestone on the way to something greater – walking. He doesn't know yet that he is capable of walking, but I do. I celebrate each accomplishment along with him, knowing just how much more he is capable of.

And so I think it is with You.

Father, You watch our spiritual growth, sharing our excitement as we blossom, knowing how much more we are capable of. Increase my desire to grow and to celebrate my accomplishments without being impatient or despairing over how much further I have to go. Help me to know that celebrating all my accomplishments alongside me and seeing me grow into who You created me to be is Your delight.

Amen.

My Mess

Heavenly Father,

I watch my son as he goes through a difficult day. He won't eat the food on his tray, he won't play independently, he just wants to be held. Last night, he didn't fall asleep until hours after his bedtime, and he woke several times. He is so much more work on days like this. It demands more of my energy after a sleepless night. He is a mess. But he is my mess.

And so I think it is with me.

Father, You are so patient with me and love me through all the spiritually difficult periods of my life. Increase my fortitude that I may be more constant in my devotion to You. Help me to know that staying with me and calling me back to Yourself during times when I am being difficult is Your delight.

Amen.

Expect More

Heavenly Father,

I watch my son as he starts cruising around the furniture. He's so proud of his accomplishment, as he should be. It's a big step, and I applaud him for it. But I know he is capable of more. I know that he will soon learn how to walk, so I challenge him by calling to him from short distances away from where he is cruising on the couch, encouraging him to leave the safety of the furniture and come to me.

And so I think it is with You.

Father, You call me out of my comfort zone to walk on water, so that I may grow in faith. Increase my courage to respond to You when You call me to do things that seem impossible. Help me to know that seeing me take these steps in faith and seeing the joy on my face once I have done so is Your delight.

Amen.

Giants

Heavenly Father,

I watch my son as he studies us. How interesting it must be for him to watch us. As a young infant who couldn't lift his head, we must have seemed like giants who were so far above him, providing his every need while living in ways that were completely foreign to him with his limited capabilities. But as he grew, he became mobile and started eating soft foods that resembled those of the giants. Then, he started pulling himself up on two feet, cruising about the furniture, and eating more of the giants' food. There must come a turning point in his young mind when he transitions from viewing us as a completely different creature to realizing, "Wait, I was made to become one of them!"

And so I think it is with me.

Father, I often look at the saints as such unobtainable ideals and such lofty giants. Increase my desire to view them as my models, and increase my belief that You created me to be one of them. Help me to know that granting me the grace to become one of them is Your delight.

Amen.

Hurt

Heavenly Father,

I watch my son as he cries in pain, blood flowing from his mouth. He was cruising along a chair when he lost his footing and fell hard on his mouth. We put what pressure he would allow us to put on it and the bleeding soon stopped, though the crying didn't. After calling the doctor to see if we needed to have him seen, and after a few days of recovery, we saw how minor this accident really was. Regardless, it still made me want to become a helicopter parent, hovering over his every move. But I know I can't do that to him. I have to let him get hurt. It is by cruising that he will learn to walk, then run. And walking and running will enable him to learn and grow in countless ways. Even so, it is hard to watch him get hurt.

And so I think it is with You.

Father, You watch me stumble and fall into sin as I try to grow spiritually; You hate to see me hurt myself when I turn from You. Increase my determination to oppose sin, that I may grow closer to You without further serious injury. Help me to know that always being there to help stop the hemorrhage and to comfort me back to health as much as I will allow You to is Your delight.

Amen.

Testing

Heavenly Father,

I watch my son as he hides behind the blinds. He looks at me as he pulls the blinds and shakes them before going behind them. He knows what will happen. I will go over and pull him away. He knows that it's against the rules. He does it to seek attention. He's testing me to see whether I'll get him again. But this time will be different. This time, I will not get him unless he is in danger, so that he learns not to seek attention by misbehaving.

And so I think it is with me.

Father, there are times when I put You to the test, wondering if You'll respond in the way I wish. Increase my trust in You, especially in times when I don't get the response from You that I want. Help me to know that seeing me understand that Your responses are out of Your infinite love for me is Your delight.

Amen.

Hide & Seek

Heavenly Father,

I watch my giggling son as he crawls into a room and closes the door behind him. I call out after him, "Where's my baby boy?" as if I don't know where he is. Even if I wasn't sure where he was, his joyful squeals would give him away. I don't have to open the door to find him, because he doesn't have the patience to hide long enough for me to open the door. He opens it, giggles, and slams the door shut in my face.

And so I think it is with me.

Father, I try to hide from You as if You couldn't find me. Increase my desire to be seen and known by You, so that I run to You from my hiding place. Help me to know that seeing me run to You to receive Your love is Your delight.

Amen.

Forbidden Cabinet

Heavenly Father,

I watch my son as he plays in the kitchen. He is allowed to play with any cabinet that is within his reach except for the one under the sink, where the garbage and poisonous cleaning supplies are stored. That one we keep locked. Even though he can play with everything in any other cabinet, what cabinet does he try to open first? The forbidden cabinet. He has a wonderful time playing with the pots, pans, and Tupperware in the other cabinets when he gets around to them, but he always goes for the forbidden cabinet first.

And so I think it is with me.

Father, I bear the imprint of concupiscence, the result of Adam and Eve's choice to eat the forbidden fruit even though they could have eaten from any other tree in the garden. Increase my desire to obey You when You forbid something, knowing that You are forbidding the poison and garbage for my own good. Help me to know that seeing me thrive when I avoid what is bad for me and turn my attention to the good is Your delight.

Amen.

Babbling

Heavenly Father,

I watch my son as he becomes an expert babbler. His range of sounds and voice inflections have greatly improved. He babbles at me, but I do not know how much of the sound he is making has meaning and how much is just noise. I speak to him, but I don't know how much he understands of what I am saying to him.

And so I think it is with me.

Father, I wonder how many times You try to speak with me only to have Your voice fall on deaf ears. Increase the attentiveness of my heart to perceive Your call. Help me to know that watching me learn the language of contemplative prayer and hearing me babble is Your delight.

Amen.

Reluctant Giver

Heavenly Father,

I watch my son as he offers me one of his baby toys and then pulls it back without letting go. He wants to give me his toy, but he hasn't figured out yet that in order to do so, he needs to let go. He holds onto it, and after pulling it back, he crawls away as if he had never offered it to me at all.

And so I think it is with me.

Father, I try to give myself to You and entrust my loved ones and concerns to You, but I don't know how to let go. Increase my surrender, that I may learn to let go of whatever is holding me back from trusting You with what is most valuable to me. Help me to know that seeing me entrust You with what I have and returning it to me tenfold is Your delight.

Amen.

Baby Food

Heavenly Father,

I watch my son as he loses his taste for baby food. He refuses to eat anything that is puréed. He swats the spoon out of my hand when I try to offer it to him. He wants to eat what his daddy and I eat, which is great, except he doesn't have enough teeth to chew most of it. I'm left scrambling to find soft foods that have the nutrients he needs to thrive.

And so I think it is with You.

Father, at times, I outrun my grace, attempting experiences I am not spiritually mature enough for, and I end up biting off more than I can chew. Increase my openness to what You are feeding me at the present moment, and increase my patience to wait for deeper things until I am spiritually mature enough to handle them. Help me to know that seeing me desire a richer, more mature spiritual life is Your delight.

Amen.

One Year

Heavenly Father,

I watch my son as he turns one year old. He has grown from a helpless baby into a small boy. He could barely control his limbs when he was first born, but he is now an efficient crawler. He only knew how to cry, but now his babbling sounds resemble speaking and his giggles are filled with joy. He was toothless and could only drink for nourishment, but he now has a few teeth and eats a wide variety of solid foods. He did not know how to communicate or interact with the world of giants, but he is getting good at hiding when we play hide-and-seek and peek-a-boo and knows how to communicate to us when he's ready to eat or to go to bed by pulling on us. He has made so much progress. What a long time it must feel like to him.

But it was really quite short. It was a small fraction of my lifetime. It was the length of time I spent in third grade or prepared for an annual competition. I lived through 18 such lifetimes before I finished high school, and I have already had my 10-year high school reunion. I have done and seen so much more than my son could ever fathom given his short life thus far.

And yet, what an impact that short life has made on myself, my husband, our parents, siblings, friends, all those who have encountered him directly, and all those who have encountered him indirectly – including all those who have read these prayers. How glad it makes my heart to think of how one little one can have so great an influence on so many lives.

And so I think it is with You.

Father, our lives are but a single breath to You, but You value each individual life and observe the beauty of how one person in Your creation affects so many others. Increase my awareness that my life has more value than I could ever imagine. Help me to know that watching how my seemingly small life has permanently changed the world You created is Your delight.

Bless us as we go forth to continue to seek Your presence in our everyday lives.

Amen.

74085603R00035

Made in the USA
Middletown, DE
19 May 2018